The Caleb Generation
Take Your Mountain, At Any Age

Steve Kelly

Table of Contents

You're never too old to dream a new dream.
– C.S. Lewis

The best way to get a husband to do something is to suggest that perhaps he is too old to do it.
– Shirley MacLaine

If wrinkles must be written on our brows, let them not be written upon the heart. The spirit should never grow old.
– James A. Garfield

It is never too late to shine; never.
– George Eliot

Introduction

Aging is an inescapable fact of life. Every single human being, if he or she is fortunate to survive beyond the age of forty, experiences a variety of emotions, sensations and physical changes that accompany a long life. Each generation experiences transformative events that shape who they are and influence how they live.

As the preceding quotes demonstrate, many heartfelt and humorous comments have been made about the stage of life that is considered "middle age" and beyond. The funny thing is, with every passing year, I keep changing the definition of middle age. Is it forty years old, halfway between birth and the current life expectancy of eighty? Is it fifty years old, halfway to one hundred? Is it sixty years old, halfway between twenty and one hundred?

Regardless of how you define getting older, this book is for you. Even if you are still in your teen years, this book can help you. If you have the right attitude, you can achieve great things. At any age.

The Caleb Generation is about refusing to settle for mediocrity. It's about ignoring the obstacles of life and focusing on God's plan for achieving greatness in and for His Kingdom.

The Caleb Generation takes its name from the great Israelite leader who joined with Joshua and gave a positive report to Moses after spying the land of Canaan, which God had promised them. Caleb encouraged the people to believe God's promises. But ten other spies focused on the size of the enemy, and the people of Israel chose to accept the negative report and collectively shrunk away from the challenge, consumed by fear.

The Caleb Generation is a term I've coined for the group of people aged 40-85, which was Caleb's lifespan from the time he first saw the Promised Land, until he finally obtained his Promised Land. This book is a rally cry for the people in that age group. To understand, as Caleb did, that aging doesn't mean slowing down.

Growing older is not a bad thing; it's a human thing. If you are a member of *the Caleb Generation*, your example of faithfulness and service to God is needed, now more than ever, by the younger generations.

In Joshua 14, after forty years of wandering the wilderness, we find Caleb sharing the story and teaching the principles of faithfulness and strength in God that sustained him and encouraged him as he was *finally* about to enter the Promised Land. He was going to finally get the mountain God promised him four decades earlier.

The Caleb Generation is about never giving up. It's about keeping your passion for the things of God *and* taking your mountain.

Don't accept second best. Don't lose your vision even when your eyesight dims. Don't leave the body of Christ when your body grows weak. Renew your strength. Rise above the negative voices and difficult circumstances you face.

As Winston Churchill said while addressing his alma mater in 1941, "Never, ever, ever, ever, ever, ever, ever give up. Never give in. Never give up. *Never give up.*"

No matter how old you are, if you have the spirit to work and the faith to believe, you can claim God's promises. You can claim your mountain. Don't abandon the dreams God put in your heart, even if decades have passed.

If you believe God isn't finished working in your life; if you believe that if you're still breathing, there's work to be done, this book is for you. You are a member of *The Caleb Generation.*

1. Plan Your Battles

Have you ever tried to run a race without spending time training in the weeks and months before the event? Have you ever taken a test without studying? Have you ever played a sport or a game without knowing the rules?

If so, you know the pain, discomfort and downright frustration of trying to do something you aren't prepared for – or worse yet – you have no passion to pursue. Unfortunately, people make this mistake regularly, and in things much more significant than a recreational activity. Frequently, our greatest discomforts in life come from self-inflicted difficulties. Too often, we jump into a situation or join a cause without analyzing all the reasons, benefits or costs associated with our decision.

Like the Israelites who listened to the negative report from the unfaithful spies, we hear a report that agitates us or elevates our emotions and before too long, we're running away from the battle God longs for us to fight. Or worse, we run headlong into a conflict we don't even understand.

As we look to Caleb's message and example, we discover wisdom that will enable us to avoid getting caught in the wrong fight. *As we read his words, we first learn the power of planning our battles:*

I was forty years old when Moses the servant of the Lord sent me from Kadesh Barnea to spy out the land, and I brought back word to him as it was in my heart.[1]

Avoid battles that don't have a Kingdom consequence.

The first and easiest filter to use in deciding whether to get involved in a conflict is whether the battle has a Kingdom consequence. Caleb was operating as a spy in this passage. He was part of the elite forces, a special operations unit of the Israelite military. He, along with eleven other leaders, went behind enemy lines at great risk because there was a very real and important Kingdom consequence to his mission.

How Caleb ended up spying the Promised Land is one of the most well-known tales of the Old Testament. The Jews were God's chosen people but they strayed from Him and worshipped foreign idols. As a consequence, the book of Exodus tells us that the Egyptians enslaved them for over 400 years.[2]

They finally escaped the Pharaoh and crossed the Red Sea through a miraculous intervention by God. He parted the waters and they crossed on dry land.[3] They were on their way to the destiny God promised Abraham over twenty generations earlier.[4]

Delivering the nation of Israel to the Promised Land was a battle with Kingdom consequence, if ever there was one. Despite repeated failures and frequent mistakes, **God's promise would eventually come to pass, and Caleb was determined to participate in God's work.**

Caleb was not intimidated by the "giants in the land"[5], because he was on a Kingdom mission. When 83% of the spies trembled in fear and told the Israelites, "We are not able to go up against the people, for they are stronger than we"[6], *Caleb alone stood before the crowd and declared a*

different message: *"Let us go up at once and take possession, for we are well able to overcome it!"*[7]

Caleb knew God was in the battle, and therefore victory was assured. A key part of planning your battles is making the clear determination that the battle you enter is one of Kingdom consequence.

Follow your leader into the fight.

Caleb was confident in God but he was also confident in the mission because he trusted his leadership. He says in Joshua 14:7, "I was forty years old when *Moses the servant of the Lord sent me…"*. Caleb rightly identifies the hierarchy that God had ordained. Interestingly, he identifies Moses as "the servant of the Lord". Caleb knew that Moses was the appointed man whom God used to lead the people of Israel. Caleb's boldness came in part from his understanding of his leader's faithfulness.

Sure, Moses made mistakes. He was human, like all leaders. In fact, Moses was prevented from actually seeing the Promised Land because of his transgressions. When Moses disobeyed God in how he obtained water for the Israelites, God barred him from entering the land his heart longed to see.[8]

Despite Moses' failings, Caleb remained obedient to Moses' leadership. Moses stumbled a time or two but Caleb saw the hand of God in his leader's steps, and faithfully followed him into the battle.

Over the years, I have seen many people lose heart when a leader makes a mistake. They often disconnect themselves from the very place and plan God had for them, because a leader failed to be perfect.

As Caleb demonstrates, the connection to leadership is paramount. He found his destiny by remaining submitted to the authority that God appointed. **Caleb discovered the promises of God when he followed his leader into the fight.**

Don't fight another person's battle.

Perhaps the most critical element in planning your battle is to make sure you're fighting *your battle.*

Caleb was fighting with and for his people. He was fighting for Kingdom consequence. He was following his leader. There was no question about his alignment. He had wandered the wilderness, had walked through the valleys of life and was standing on the promises of God, alongside his family. There was no disputing that this was where he belonged.

Yet, there were plenty of disputes all around him that he refused to take on as his own. When others doubted, grumbled and rebelled, Caleb held on to his faith in God and remained unaffected by the quarreling in his midst. The Israelites repeatedly questioned their leadership and even God, yet there is no record of Caleb joining in the gripe fest.

In fact, in Joshua 14:8, Caleb says that even when his brothers made the people quiver in fear, *"I wholly followed the Lord my God."*

What a powerful testimony! Caleb was faithful to God even when others failed.

If only we could all be like Caleb. The next time you hear the murmuring of fellow believers, will you be like Caleb? Will you wholly follow God? Will you ignore the cynics and the critics and stand firm for Christ?

Too often, a complainer attracts others and before long, there's a big fight that consumes the workers and prevents us from entering the real battle that God is asking us to fight.

Many times I've heard a complaint from someone in church and thought, "that sounds terrible." I've learned to avoid commenting or making a decision until I hear the whole story. As a pastor, I've discovered there are three sides to every argument. There's the first two sides, proclaimed by each person in the disagreement, then there's a third side, which is the truth.

Proverbs 18:17 explains this phenomenon when talking about legal proceedings. "*The first to present his case seems right,* until another comes forward and questions him." As a pastor, I've discovered the truth of this verse many times.

The next time someone asks you to take up arms in a conflict, ask yourself if (1) it's a battle with Kingdom consequence; (2) your leader is calling you to fight; and (3) it's the battle *you* are supposed to fight.

If not, turn to Jesus' example in Luke 12:13-14. Jesus was approached by two brothers in a quarrel and Jesus asked, "who made me a judge or arbitrator over you?" **Jesus refused to get involved because it wasn't a fight with Kingdom consequence and it wasn't His battle.**

Instead of getting involved in someone else's battle, encourage them to follow the order of Jesus' instruction in Matthew 18. Jesus taught us to handle disputes in the following order:

- **Discuss it directly with the individual. (v. 15)**
- **Discuss it with two or three people, *if* you fail to reconcile in the first conversation. (v. 16)**
- **If, after discussing it directly, then with**

**two or three others, there is still no recon-
ciliation, *then* take it to the church body.
(v. 17)**

Avoiding other people's battles is a significant part of being a member of the Caleb generation. Plan your battles
by aligning them with Kingdom consequence, under the
direction of your leader. You will find passion and strength
for the fight. Turn the page to read about a figure from
American history who planned his battles. An honorary
member of the *Caleb Generation,* ***Ulysses S. Grant.***

Ulysses S. Grant
(1822-1885)[9]

Ulysses S. Grant was a Civil War general for the North and became the 18th President of the United States. Long before those achievements, President Grant suffered difficult periods and learned valuable lessons.

Like all members of the *Caleb Generation*, he didn't discover his true potential until he reached his 40s and beyond.

He graduated from West Point at the age of 21 and fought in the Mexican War in 1846-48. He married Julia B. Dent in 1848. He was sent to a military post in California from 1852-54, without his wife and two young sons. Depressed by living apart from his family, Grant resigned his commission and began working on a farm near St. Louis, Missouri.

For eight years, the balance of his 30s, Grant struggled in many ways. Without the disciplined life of the military, he failed to stay on task and quickly proved to be a poor businessman. He struggled with alcoholism and was generally in a miserable place, physically and spiritually.

He belonged in the fight. He was a soldier and civilian life was clearly a mistake. When the Civil War erupted, he was called to become a Colonel in the 21st Illinois Infantry, just a few months shy of his fortieth birthday. Within ten weeks, President Lincoln petitioned Congress to elevate Grant to the rank of Brigadier General.

Grant continued his meteoric rise through the ranks of US Army leadership over the course of the Civil War, culminating in accepting General Robert E. Lee's surrender on April 9, 1865, ending the Civil War, and finally abolishing slavery in the United States.

Grant was later made the first Four-Star General in U.S. history. Four years after the Civil War ended, he was elected President of the United States, and served two terms.

One of the hallmarks of Grant's leadership was his tenacious will and his strategic planning. How does Grant gain entrance into the *Caleb Generation?*

1. **He fought a battle with Kingdom consequence.** God's heart for justice compels freedom for all. Ending slavery in the United States certainly qualifies as a battle with "Kingdom consequence".

2. **He followed his leader into the fight.** Like Caleb, Grant's submission to leadership enabled him to reach his goal. President Lincoln called him to serve, and he did so faithfully. When others complained of Grant's shortcomings (like the Israelites did with Moses), President Lincoln simply said, *"I can't spare this man, he fights."*

3. **He didn't fight other people's battles.** Ulysses S. Grant was uncompromising and unflinching in his conviction to fight the Civil War. His singular attention to the big picture of winning the war prevented him

from engaging in political disputes with other military leaders. This trait won him few friends, *but it won the war*. He knew every minute spent focused on petty disagreements was a minute wasted. So focused was Ulysses S. Grant, that a Union soldier is reported to have said, "Ulysses don't scare worth a damn!"[10] after he received orders from General Grant while bombs were exploding all around them.

Much has been written about Ulysses S. Grant's greatness. Many have criticized him for his moral weaknesses; despite all his struggles and in spite of all the criticism, Ulysses S. Grant stands as one of the greatest leaders in American history because he didn't give up. At an age when some people would think he was past his prime, Grant planned his battles. And won. For his conviction and his faithfulness, Ulysses S. Grant deserves to be a member of the *Caleb Generation.*

2. Swim against the Tide

Holding on to a belief when the vast majority of people disagree with you is one of the most difficult things to do in life. Even when you are confident in a position, if someone close to you challenges your assertion, it's hard not to second-guess yourself.

Yet, Caleb didn't second-guess his convictions even when the overwhelming majority of spies disagreed with him. **Even when the entire nation of Israel ignored his recommendation, he did not waver.** He describes his action as bringing a report to Moses "as it was in my heart."[11]

If the twelve spies' mission was like most military operations, there would have been discussion and preparation among the spies before delivering the report to Moses and the nation of Israel. The significance of the operation cannot be overstated. The Israelites had escaped the terrible oppression of the Egyptians and were on their way to *finally* inhabiting God's Promised Land. Given the extreme importance of the moment, it seems very likely that the spies had an internal discussion before returning to headquarters.

Perhaps the conversation went something like this (Names used are the actual names of the spies, as recorded in Numbers 13):

Palti: *Those are some huge people in that country. Did you see the size of those soldiers?*

Sethur: *I sure did! Holy cow! There is no way we can take those guys out. Even if we had the army of Egypt, which we don't, I still think we'd lose.*

Caleb: *Aren't you forgetting that **we** already defeated the Egyptian Army? Our God is able to deliver these people into our hands as well.*

Joshua: *That's right, Caleb. I agree with you.*

Igal: *You guys are out of your minds! Such dreamers! We are to give a report to Moses, and we have to base it on the facts. The circumstances around us are pretty clear – the Canaanites are massive, and we are puny grasshoppers compared to them!*

Caleb: *Yes, but faith is bigger than circumstances. God is bigger than all of the Canaanites.*

Shammua: *I don't even know why you are arguing with us.*

Here, by show of hands, how many believe we should attack the Canaanites?

{Only Joshua and Caleb raise their hands}

Shammua: *I think it's pretty clear, Caleb. By a vote of 10 to 2, your position is refuted.*

Caleb: *It's not my position; it's God's position. It's what He wants, it's what He promised us!*

Shammua: *Listen, Caleb, we are going to give this report. I am from the tribe of Reuben, it's my responsibility to issue the official report and it's going to say that while the land is full of plenty and is clearly prosperous, the people of Canaan are too strong and fortified for us to overcome. Therefore, we should not enter into battle with them.*

Caleb: *Well, I'm from the tribe of Judah, and I can promise you before this is all over, we're going to have something to say about the fulfillment of God's promises.*

Maybe the conversation thousands of years ago wasn't identical to the dialogue above, but there is no doubt Caleb was tested. His resolve and his commitment to what He knew God wanted was challenged. First, by the men in his company, and then by the enormous crowd. Only

Joshua agreed with him, and even Joshua did not speak (according to Numbers 13) when the people decided to listen to the negative report.

It couldn't have been easy for Caleb to stand before everyone and speak his mind. Yet he did.

In your life, moments of testing will come. There will be circumstances that challenge your faith in God. There will be crises that arise; physical difficulties, financial stress, relationship trauma, etc. In all these things, we must be like Caleb. **We must be not just willing, but also able, to swim against the tide.**

It's one thing to want to swim against the tide, but it's another thing to be able to. Caleb used a word that is mentioned throughout the Bible – "heart". The Hebrew word, *lebab*, as used by Caleb, is defined as "the inner man, mind, will, soul or understanding."[12] The word implies a deep and settled, immovable conviction. It also implies the core element of all members of the *Caleb Generation*: FAITH.

Without faith it is impossible to please God.[13] Without

faith, it is impossible to be a member of the *Caleb Generation*.

Despite the staggeringly large number of people who disputed Caleb's opinion and who refused to accept his report, Caleb never changed his mind because he was convinced in his heart that God would give Israel the victory. The deep resolve in his heart gave him the ability to swim against the tide that all leaders face in some way during their life, the tide of popular opinion.

In the New Testament, the apostle Paul writes in Galatians 6:9, "Do not grow weary in doing good, for in due season we shall reap if we *do not lose **heart**.*"

Just like Caleb, Paul understood that through every circumstance and every season, the difference maker between someone who thrives and someone who falls by the wayside is a matter of heart. Settle in your heart that you are following God no matter what. Draw strength from the example of Caleb, who endured scoffing and mocking and outright rejection by millions of people. He truly swam against the tide. You can too.

George Edward Foreman
(1949-)[14]

George Edward Foreman is perhaps best known by young people as the seller of the George Foreman Grill, a fat-reducing meat cooker that sold over 100 million units in the fifteen years after it was launched. But, to members of the *Caleb Generation*, George Foreman is remembered as a heavyweight boxer who fought in the heyday of pugilism. When names like Ali and Frazier dominated the sports world, Foreman stood toe to toe with the best, and for a few periods, held the undisputed heavyweight championship belt.

In 1968, he won the gold medal in the Mexico City Olympic Games. From 1969-72, Foreman won all 37 of his boxing matches (34 by KO). He was a frightening force in the boxing ring. His success earned him a shot at the championship in Kingston, Jamaica, against heavy-weight champ Joe Frazier.

Foreman won the title by TKO, after knocking Frazier down six times in two rounds.

In 1977, after a serious illness and what Foreman claimed was a near-death experience, he asked Jesus to save him. He became a Christian, stopped boxing and was ordained as a minister.

For the next ten years, Foreman dedicated himself to the ministry. He opened a youth center in Houston, Texas, and led a congregation of believers.

The next chapter in his life is a remarkable illustration of the power of a *Caleb Generation* member. In a sport domi-nated (like most sports) by the power and vigor of young men, George Foreman announced, at the age of 38, that he was returning to the boxing ring. Many warned that it was dangerous and could even be deadly, for a man of his age to fight again. What happened over the next seven years likely surprised even George Foreman.

He climbed through the ranks once again and got a title shot in 1991, at the age of 42, against Evander Holyfield. Though he didn't win, Foreman lasted all twelve rounds against the champ, and earned the respect of the critics.

Three years later, Foreman represented the *Caleb Generation* in a big way. He swam against the tide and was given a chance to fight Michael Moorer, who was nineteen years younger than the now 45-year-old Foreman. In a staggering upset, Foreman, who was losing in every round entering the tenth round, mounted a furious comeback that culminated in a devastating punch that split Moorer's lip and knocked him out cold.

Just like that, George Edward Foreman was the heavyweight champ of the world. Twenty years after losing his title for the first time, he became the oldest boxer to win the World Heavyweight Championship. As he announced to all of the naysayers, part of his motivation in going against all odds to become the champ again was his desire to "prove that age 40 is not a death sentence."

Foreman did far more than that. He proved the power of

courage, of *heart*. In every fight, he withstood numerous blows from younger fists and loud negative commentaries from older critics. If anyone represents the ability of the *Caleb Generation* to swim against the tide, it's George Foreman. For this reason, and for the delicious food prepared the world over on his ubiquitous grilling machine, George Foreman is a member of the *Caleb Generation*.

3. Understand Negativity

Some people are so negative, if you put them in a dark room, they develop. Have you ever been around someone who seems to focus on the dark clouds and never the silver linings? If you spend any measure of time with them, you begin to notice the bad things in life and ignore the good. You begin to lose your passion and drive to pursue big dreams.

This effect is the power of negativity. It is important to be aware of the life-sapping drain that negativity produces in the atmosphere. If you are going to be a member of the *Caleb Generation*, you have to avoid negativity at all costs. For you never know until it's too late what negativity may cost you.

Caleb knew the power of negativity. He knew all too well what it cost. He watched for forty years, as the Jews wandered in the wilderness, until every member of his generation died. You see, **for each and every one of his peers,** friends and acquaintances, all of those who accepted the report of the ten spies, negativity extracted the exorbitant cost of exclusion from God's Promised Land.

In Joshua 14:8, Caleb describes the impact of negativity. He declares that the report from the bad spies caused "the hearts of the people to melt."

In the previous chapter of this book, the heart is defined, as Caleb intended, as the core of a person. It is the deepest part of a person; their essence. The strength of a person's heart is also inextricably linked to the depth of their faith.

In this case, the negative report caused the heart of *literally every single adult in the entire country except Caleb and Joshua to melt and to abandon their faith in God!*

This is nearly incomprehensible. Was there no one who believed Caleb? Even the most unrealistic visionaries can typically find a few people who will join their quest, no matter how crazy. Yet, such was the palpable power of the negativity spread by the ten spies that no one was able to resist it. And so, the power of negativity yielded a loss of faith, which brought a vengeful and swift judgment from God.

Once the negativity took hold, there was no turning back. In Numbers 14, after the Israelites "wept all night" and complained against Moses, Caleb once again tried to stir their faith. He tried to return courage to their collective heart. He told the congregation that the Lord "will bring us into the land and give it to us...Only do not rebel against the Lord, nor fear the people of the land...the Lord is with us. *Do not fear them.*" [15]

What do you suppose was the response to Caleb's urging? Perhaps the people reconsidered and were moved to stir their faith? No. Not even close. Instead of returning to God's plan, the Israelites shouted their desire to *stone Caleb.* Only a miraculous intervention by God prevented them from killing Caleb[16]. So powerful is negativity, like a deadly virus, it spreads from person to person until, in this case, an entire nation was infected.

God appears and is so incensed by the Israelites that He tells Moses, "I will strike them with the pestilence and disinherit them, and I will make of you a nation."[17]

Moses responds by pleading for God to show mercy. In Numbers 14:11-25, Moses and God engage in a negotiation, of sorts. After Moses explains why God shouldn't kill the Israelites (mostly by telling God if He killed His people, the foreign nations would say that God couldn't do what He promised), God relents. He tells Moses that He will spare the nation of Israel but that "because all these men who have seen My glory…and have not heeded My voice, **they certainly shall not see the land of which I swore to their fathers, nor shall any of those who rejected Me see it.** *But My servant Caleb, because he has a different spirit in him and has followed me fully, I will bring into the land where he went, and his descendants shall inherit it.*"[18]

Isn't it interesting that God said Caleb "has a different spirit"? God was focused on the inner part of Caleb – his heart. The part of Caleb that God identified as his distinguishing feature was Caleb's source of faith that didn't waver in adversity, and didn't melt with fear.

It's clear by now that negativity is devastating. It's a deadly, corrupting power that is easy to unleash and difficult to stop. **Making the right choice about the company you**

keep is the most important thing you can do to avoid being influenced by negativity.

In the midst of a congregation, it is vital to remember that not everyone who is with you is *really with you*. There are many people who seem to be committed to what God is doing, like the nation of Israel after they fled Egypt. But, like the Israelites, we've all seen people who flinch and falter at the first sign of difficulty, even when God has clearly delivered them every step of the journey.

Typically, the negative attitude in church manifests itself through mockery. The longer a mocker is allowed to infiltrate clusters of people, the more damaging his influence will be. The book of Proverbs talks about how important it is to remove a mocker immediately.

Drive out the mocker and out goes the strife; quarrels and insults will stop.[19]

This is a non-negotiable. If you want quarrels to end, if you want insults and name-calling to cease, you must drive out the mocker. Don't try to reconcile with them; don't try to counsel them. REMOVE THEM.

Remember the Israelites. Every single person except Caleb was forbidden from receiving God's promises because they allowed a negative, mocking spirit to influence them through the report of the ten bad spies. It doesn't take very many people spewing negativity to destroy a community.

If the Jewish people lost their way after crossing the Red Sea on dry land, don't be foolish enough to think you can overcome the power of negativity and "work" with the person who is the source of the mockery. Let them go. If you must, make them go.

To be an effective member of the *Caleb Generation* you must:

1. **Understand the power of negativity**
2. **Identify it in your midst**
3. **Quickly eliminate it**

The next time someone around you starts to spread the spirit of negativity, remember the extraordinary loss that came to the Israelites as a result of tolerating and believing it. Do you want to lose all that God has promised you? Of course not. Be ruthless in your defense of the atmosphere. Be like Caleb. Regardless of the negative report of others, stand firm in your faith, keep heart, and remember the power of negativity.

Clive Staples "C.S." Lewis[20]
(1898-1963)

C.S. Lewis is widely recognized by Christians and non-Christians, by fans and critics, as one of the most brilliant thinkers, writers, and Christian apologists of the twentieth century. He was born in Ireland in 1898. His mother died when he was only ten years old, after which he was educated in English boarding schools. He came of age during World War I, and served in the British Army. He was wounded during fighting in the Somme Valley in France.

Lewis was an absolutely brilliant man. During his time as a student at Oxford University, he won multiple awards and upon graduation, become a Fellow and Tutor in English Literature.

During the next twenty years, he would form a close

and deep friendship with another famous British author, J.R.R. Tolkien, the creator of *The Hobbit* and *The Lord of the Rings*.

Lewis and Tolkien met every week with a group of fellow writers and thinkers. They called themselves "The Inklings" and they hung out in a small British pub discussing book ideas, philosophy, languages and literature. During these sessions, the men often critiqued each other's work and prodded each other in pursuit of their goals.

Tolkien and Lewis were closer to each other than any of the others, perhaps because they were each regarded as possessing an intelligence that was wildly beyond the normal person. Besides their genius, they truly complemented each other in personality. Tolkien was earnest, sincere and a very strict follower of self-imposed rules. Lewis was emotional, fun-loving and liked to break a rule now and then.

Their relationship has been discussed and written about for years but one significant detail has rarely been mentioned. This detail is very important for the purposes of the *Caleb Generation* and it demonstrates why C.S. Lewis understood the power of negativity.

The following quote from literary critic and author Laura Miller provides a context: "The fastidious Tolkien was… annoyed by Lewis' authorial sloppiness, his uncorrected mistakes and inconsistencies, which were…the result of an endearingly wholehearted forward momentum that blithely swept over the sort of minor problems that would inevitably trip up Tolkien."[21]

C.S. Lewis knew that Tolkien was a harsh critic of both himself and others. He admired the diligence of his friend, but C.S. Lewis had a different destiny. Because he understood the power of Tolkien's negativity, C.S. Lewis never read any drafts of *The Chronicles of Narnia* to Tolkien (or any of his other writing group friends) before it was published.[22]

The beloved *Narnia* series, which has been a world-wide best seller sixty years after its first printing, was too far outside the boundaries as Tolkien saw things. It had a random Santa Claus showing up giving the Pevensie children presents in the middle of a made-up world, after all. Tolkien was rigid in his opinion regarding the structure of stories and the creation of sub-worlds like Narnia.

Even though they had worked together for twenty years, were close friends and reviewed each other's work frequently, Lewis knew that Tolkien would push negative thoughts and perceptions toward Narnia. C.S. understood the power of negativity and avoided it because his inspiration for *Narnia* was too important to allow it to be harmed by Tolkien's harshly critical nature.

As a result of his understanding of the power of negativity, the world has a remarkable fable that children and adults alike love and many have said point to the love and redemption of Jesus Christ. And he wrote the entire set of seven books in only two years!

C.S. Lewis is a definite member of the *Caleb Generation*. He understood the power of negativity and wouldn't allow even his well-meaning and very close friend to bring any negativity into contact with his dream. Sometimes even family and friends have to be excluded in order for you to achieve what God wants through your life. Next time you have a blossoming idea, think carefully about who you share it with, if anyone. Remember this example. Understand the power of negativity and avoid it at all costs.

4. Keep Your Passion

Chapter 2 of this book opened with a question about entering a contest or race without training. Clearly, training is important to any venture's success. Whether it's military operations, athletic contests, legal arguments or the political arena, if a person hasn't trained before the big event, he or she will struggle and ultimately fail.

Perhaps even more important than training is undertaking an activity whole-heartedly. Keeping passion is essential for long-term achievement. Without determination and full-fledged dedication, even the most talented fail. Perhaps your passion has waned. One sign of this is when minor inconveniences begin to annoy you. Re-fire your passion and remember endurance is essential to scaling your mountain.

Talent without tenacity is nothing more than a fireworks show. The members of the *Caleb Generation* have to pursue God's plans whole-heartedly.

Many people enter middle age with their eye already looking toward retirement. While it's essential to prepare for the later days of life and to build up an inheritance for your children and grandchildren, it is a terrible shame to see people trudge through their productive years because their whole heart isn't in their day-to-day work.

Caleb knew how important it was to remain passionate about the things of God. He didn't allow insecurity and fear to prevent him from achieving his destiny. Right after the bad spies infected all of his relatives and friends, he said, "I, however, followed the Lord my God wholeheartedly." There's that word again: *heart*. This word is clearly essential to all members of the *Caleb Generation*.

Countless expressions exist about the human heart. Here are a few to consider:

The heart sees what is invisible to the eye. – H. Jackson Brown, Jr.

Though an army besiege me, my heart will not fear. – David, Psalm 27:3

They will have no fear of bad news; their hearts are steadfast, trusting the Lord. – David, Psalm 112:7

You change your life by changing your heart. – Max Lucado

The heart. The source of life. The center of man. So much has been said and written about the heart, it's certainly possible entire libraries could be constructed simply for content dealing with matters of the heart. The heart, for purposes of this chapter, is synonymous with passion.

Caleb had a passion for the things of God. This passion overcame all distractions, all critics, all negativity. This passion enabled him to say "…here I am today, eighty-five years old! I am still as strong today as the day Moses sent me out."[23]

Caleb's passion enabled him to keep his strength. It helped him keep up with the rising generation. In fact, it helped him lead the rising generation. Passion transcends age, experience, and demographic categories. When young people see an older person with passion, they are inspired and they will follow. **Today's young people long to be** influenced by the *Caleb Generation*. They don't want to hear speeches or read old books. They want to see the passion of God burning within their parents and grandparents. They want to see the *Caleb Generation* worshipping and serving God actively.

The transition from generation to generation in leadership causes many churches, companies and communities to flounder. As the baton is passed, people often stumble or lose their place altogether. **When the *Caleb Generation* pursues God wholeheartedly, this transition is smooth and it leads to exponential growth and genuine fulfillment of each generation's calling.**

The *Caleb Generation* is called to lead the rising generations and the future of God's work is dependent on this mentoring and modeling.

Perhaps you feel like you can't connect to the rising generation. You don't have to connect to them; you have to connect to God. When you pursue God wholeheartedly, He brings the connection that will enable an honoring, powerful relationship to be established between the generations.

Here are some time-tested suggestions for keeping your passion and inspiring the next generation:

- Attend church. Serve, don't just sit.

- Worship God with your whole heart. Regardless of the volume of the music or the beat, *worship God.*

- Don't be the last in and first out of a church service. Linger. Make friends.

- Cheer on the next generation.

- Celebrate and promote achievements that exhibit endurance. (e.g., long-term marriage)

- Run your race. Every day, pursue God with your whole heart.

Caleb kept his passion. He followed God wholeheartedly. It didn't matter how he felt, what the circumstances presented, or what others believed. He followed God and he kept his passion. Follow God wholeheartedly. Make the *Caleb Generation proud. Keep your passion.*

The next honorary member of the *Caleb Generation* is someone who kept his passion in spite of how long it took for his vision to come to pass. Be inspired and pick up that dream you put on the shelf. Return to your passion and you will see God invigorate your life.

J.R.R. Tolkien[24]
(1892-1973)

John Ronald Reuel Tolkien is best known for his hugely popular books, *The Hobbit* and *The Lord of the Rings*, which have been adapted into blockbuster movies over the past decade. He was a preeminent scholar of the English language, and professor at Oxford University with his good friend and colleague, C.S. Lewis.

J.R.R. Tolkien was a brilliant man, a faithful husband and father, and a devout Catholic. As for his affiliation with the *Caleb Generation*, Tolkien belongs because of his ability to keep his passion.

He was a "philologist", a student of languages. He was so obsessed with the history and development of languages that he actually made up several languages. He decided that a language isn't real unless someone actually speaks it, so he created Middle Earth, the universe in which *The Lord of the Rings* is set, so that the characters in the book could speak his language! One thing is certain, Tolkien was not an ordinary man.

He was so passionate about his work, as mentioned in the previous chapter, he kept working and working to make it better. He was never satisfied with simply finishing his stories. They had to be perfect.

The Hobbit was published in 1937. It was so successful, Tolkien's publisher called him and asked for more. Tolkien began working on *The Lord of the Rings*. Most books in a series are published within a year or two, at most, of the initial book's printing. In fact, in recent years, some publishers have released two or three books at once, with the hope of exciting the audience with the opportunity to have the "whole story" without waiting.

In the case of *The Lord of the Rings*, the sequel to *The Hobbit*, it was not one year, or two, or even ten. **Sixteen years passed between *The Hobbit* and the publishing of *The Lord of the Rings*.**

That's right, sixteen years! By the time *The Lord of the Rings* was on the bookstore shelves, Tolkien was sixty years old! He painstakingly worked at his story over more than a decade and a half. It doesn't matter what your job is, it takes passion to keep at it for sixteen years. Along the way, there were many opportunities to abandon the work. People asked if anyone would even remember *The Hobbit* by the time *The Lord of the Rings* was finished, and rightly so.

Yet, it was a runaway success. Among English language novels, only Charles Dickens' *A Tale of Two Cities* has sold more copies, and it was printed nearly one hundred years earlier.[25] The trilogy of movies made in 2001-2003 grossed over one billion dollars at the box office.

Many people would have given up. Most people would have lost their passion. Tolkien never did. The flame burned in him to create a story that matched his vision. He kept honing and editing and fixing the book until it aligned itself with his passion. For his ability to keep his passion alive and publish one of the world's most beloved books (mainly by younger people) at age sixty, J.R.R.

Tolkien has earned the right to be called a part of the *Caleb Generation*.

5. GO

Have you ever read about a place that you'd like to visit? Maybe you've even watched videos of an exotic destination with crystal blue waters and sparkling white beaches. Maybe you've heard others tell of a trip to tall mountains and remote forests. You can imagine, you can watch, you can learn all about those places but until you physically enter that water or climb that mountain or wander on an isolated nature trail, you don't really know what it's like. You can't really have understanding, or a truly personal ownership of the experience until you go.

Something happens when you go to a place. You can see it more clearly, you can breathe the air, you can touch the soil. How many times has a friend tried to explain a place and they can't? They say, "You just have to go there."

The same is true about God's promises. You can't have them until you go there.

In Joshua 14:9, Caleb received the knowledge of this truth when Moses swore to him, "The land on which your feet have walked will be your inheritance and that of your children forever, because you have followed the Lord my God wholeheartedly."

God promised Caleb that he would have all the land *on which his feet walked*. If Caleb hadn't gone anywhere, he wouldn't have any land for himself and his children.

In order to see God's promises fulfilled in your life, you have to be willing to go.

Years ago, I experienced this reality first hand. I was a young man, just getting started in the ministry. I was serving in the church where I found Jesus. At the time, our church was meeting in a rented warehouse. We didn't own any land. We didn't own any buildings. Like the Israelites, we were still not living in the fullness of God's plan.

The senior pastor knew this and he had a vision for the church to acquire property and build a church. When he first proposed this to the congregation, there wasn't a very enthusiastic agreement. The people were comfortable in our rented warehouse -- a tiny spot, without room for growth. They didn't really mind that the church wasn't taking ground for the future generations.

The senior pastor refused to accept this limited view. He came up with a plan to engage the congregation. **He knew that sometimes, for things to make sense, for people to really understand, they have to go there.**

He announced one Sunday morning that he had contacted the owners of a thirty-acre parcel of land. He had gotten permission for the church to go out to the property and mow the grass.

Every family from our church was assigned a quarter acre or so to mow. The next week, we all put on our work clothes, loaded up trucks full of lawnmowers and went out to the land. Fathers, mothers, grandmothers, teenagers…everybody got involved. Everybody walked the land, pushing lawnmowers. As we were out there, clearing the vegetation, we all began to see what the senior pastor saw. We could have our own land! We wouldn't have to pay rent anymore. We could build something that would last. Something that our children and grandchildren could have and carry on the purposes of God.

Once we went there, everything changed. Shortly after the mowing party, we got permission to hold a tent meeting on the property. The church sprang to life, full of passion for God, and full of vision for the property. Eventually, we acquired the property and built a church for God's glory. But none of it would have happened if we didn't first *go*.

Before we went there, our senior pastor had already been there in his mind. Our thoughts can take us wherever we are going before our bodies catch up. **Where are your thoughts taking you?**

Do you allow your thoughts to take you away from God's best? Or do you take your negative thoughts captive and focus on God's promises? The Israelites lost focus on who God was and what He had promised. They listened to the negative report, they complained about their problems. As a result, the Israelites did not get to go. Only Caleb did, because he went there with his thoughts. He believed and followed God. Sometimes everything around you looks and sounds like the end is near. That's when you most need to allow your thoughts to take you to God's truth. That's when you need to use your thoughts to GO.

When Sharon and I were just starting in ministry, we didn't have a spare nickel. Like lots of young couples, we had no money and few examples of how to manage money. Our first year, we ate ham and cheese sandwiches almost every night. I can't eat ham and cheese sandwiches anymore. If I see a ham and cheese sandwich, I practically break out in hives.

One day, I got tired of the ham and cheese. More importantly, I got tired of our poverty mindset. We made a conscious decision to put ourselves in places that were nice; places that were representative of God's blessings. Sharon and I began to visit nice restaurants and hotels. We were intimidated at first. We didn't know all the proper manners. We could only afford to get a juice or a sandwich. We weren't trying to spend a bunch of money, which we didn't have anyway. We were trying to get comfortable in our future. We knew God had promised us a great future, and we knew we had to *go there* to get it.

So we did. We started to change our thoughts about wealth. We changed our words. Instead of saying "We can't afford it," we began to say, "we choose not to buy it right now." We were in charge of our finances, not the other way around.

Before too long, we began to see ourselves in nice places, living blessed. We began to manage our money properly. And God expanded our influence and blessing.

Like Caleb, we knew that God would give us everywhere our feet tread. We just had to go there.

If you want to have a better marriage, go to a place that will help you. Go to a marriage seminar, or go to a counselor who can help you strengthen your most important earthly relationship.

If you want a better business, go to experts who can help take you there. Go to conferences that will enable you to get to where you want your business to go.

If you've been cooped up, intimidated or fearful of breaking out of financial limitations, health restrictions or relationship constraints, I encourage you to just GO. Be like Caleb. Be a member of the *Caleb Generation*. *Get up and GO.*

The next profile of a *Caleb Generation* legend is someone who literally had to go out of this world. Check out the story of Neil Armstrong on the next page.

Neil Alden Armstrong[26]
(1930-2012)

Neil Alden Armstrong grew up in Ohio. He attended Purdue University on a US Navy scholarship, where he studied aeronautical engineering. He was plucked away from his classes to fight in the Korean War, where he flew 78 combat missions.

He survived the war, and returned to college, where he continued to develop his knowledge of his lifelong fascination, flight. After college, he joined the National Advisory Committee for Aeronautics, the organization that would become NASA.

He was obsessed with flying farther, faster. He imagined the day when man could be able to fly beyond the Earth's atmosphere. Perhaps he knew that he would one day be able to experience it. When NASA announced its astronaut program, he jumped in with both feet, eager to fly in a way beyond what most people could comprehend.

In 1962, he joined the astronaut program. A year earlier, President John F. Kennedy had proclaimed the goal of putting a man on the moon "by the end of the decade". The President's vision matched Armstrong's passion, and he couldn't wait to *go there*.

When JFK was assassinated on November 22, 1963, the vision took on a new level of intensity. Everyone in NASA was sold out to fulfill the President's dream.

For seven grueling years, they labored and learned, all the while committed to eventually *going there*.

They suffered setbacks along the way. It's possible many people wanted to give up. According to historians, the scale and scope of the effort to put a man on the moon was rivaled only by the construction of the Panama Canal and the Manhattan Project, which created the atomic bomb.

With just a few months remaining on President Kennedy's timeline, the Apollo 11 took off from the launch pad at Kennedy Space Center. Commander Armstrong, along with Michael Collins and Edwin "Buzz" Aldrin were on their way.

At 10:56 PM EST, on July 20, four days after they left Earth, Neil Armstrong exited the Lunar Module and declared, "That's one small step for man, one giant leap for mankind." After going there over and over in his mind, he went there. Physically, tangibly, fully.

After years of planning and thinking, it all came to pass. From the President's vision to the NASA engineers and scientists' planning to the astronauts' flying, the people went there and history was made. Indeed, civilization itself was changed.

As part of the *Caleb Generation*, Neil Armstrong embodies the principle, *GO*, unlike any other.

6. God's Promises

This book is intended to fill the reader with hope and courage. The message of the *Caleb Generation* is that you're never too old to accomplish what God has promised you. This is partly true because God is not constrained by age. He's not limited by the human body. While it's true that aging brings physical changes and needs, it's also true that God's promises will help keep you alive. Indeed, God's promises can actually bring life itself.

One of the most astonishing examples of this occurs long before Caleb showed up. Way back, near the very beginning of the Bible, two old people were living and wondering when and how God would fulfill His promises.

Abraham, the father of the nation that birthed Caleb, was obedient to God. God promised him that He would make Abraham "into a great nation."[27] Of course, in order to become a great nation, Abraham had to have children. Regardless of how long it takes to have enough heirs to build a nation, there's one piece to the puzzle that is essential. Heirs. Offspring. Children.

Picking up the story of Abraham and his wife, Sarah, years later, we discover they are still without children. In Genesis 17, God speaks to Abraham and once again promises him that He will make a great nation of him.

Abraham laughed. Why? Because Abraham was ninety-nine years old and his wife was ninety. Even in the days when people lived a bit longer, Abraham and Sarah were past the point of having children. Yet, even at their advanced age they did indeed have a son, Isaac, whose twelve sons became the twelve tribes of Israel.

God's promises are uncontestable. They are irrefutable. They are unstoppable. **No matter how much time lapses, no matter what the natural order dictates, when God makes a covenant, He keeps it**.

This is the power of God's promises for the *Caleb Generation*: to know that He will not fail. He cannot fail. He will deliver to you what He has promised. It's a guarantee.

Caleb knew that God would keep His promises. ***God's promises will keep you young and alive, so remember them regularly. They will refresh you and strengthen*** *you, just like Caleb.*

Caleb said, "Now then, just as the Lord promised, He has kept me alive for forty-five years, since the time He said this to Moses, while Israel moved about in the desert."[28]

One of the most powerful parts of that verse is the following line: *since the time He said this to Moses*. God said it forty-five years earlier, in Numbers 14. From that moment, Caleb held on to the promise that God gave him. For over four decades of wandering and waffling and the wasting away of a generation, Caleb stood firm, confident of the truth that if God promised, it would be.

What an impressive faith. Caleb's faith and heart was stronger than perhaps his ancestor Abraham, who laughed at God's promise. Caleb was eighty-five when he made the declaration above, and though his promise wasn't about having children, it was no less unnatural.

The land was promised to Caleb, but he would still have to fight for it. He was eighty-five. Fighting is a young man's game. When Caleb and the spies went to scout the land, he was forty. He was in his prime, ready to go to war. Now, he was an old man. He probably should have been asking for help finding his cane.

Perhaps Caleb fought all the harder because time was running out. He knew that he was fighting for future generations. God had promised the land to Caleb and his heirs.

So, Caleb entered the Promised Land, ready to fight, ready to get all that God promised him. If you find yourself forgetting the promises of God because "too much" time has passed since He first made His promise, take a look at Caleb. Remember God's promises. They will be fulfilled. They will keep you young and alive.

WILLIAM KELLY[29]
(1929-2008)

The story of William Kelly isn't one, like some of the other honorary *Caleb Generation* members in this book, that can be found in the history books. But, his life and his legacy was no less significant. In fact, in the priorities of Heaven, the life of William Kelly is one of great significance.

William Kelly is my father. He was an Irishman, raising his family of five kids with my mother, Betty, in Queens, New York. He owned a pub in the Bronx. Unfortunately, my father and my mother were alcoholics, and Dad was a gambler. When I was eight years old, because of the troubles my dad's addictions got him into, we moved to Sydney, Australia. I'll never forget standing at the airport in New York, when I swore to myself that I'd return to the

United States one day.

On our trip to Australia, my mother got so intoxicated, she lay down in the aisle floor. The airplane captain threatened to kick us off the plane. My family was very dysfunctional and my parents' alcoholism caused tremendous heartache and pain for all of us.

But, the story doesn't end there. Thank God! My father had a good friend, Mr. Keehan, who was his drinking buddy. Mr. Keehan had a son, Gerard, who became my best friend as a result of our fathers' relationship. Gerard invited me to church and I became a Christian as a 17 year-old boy.

Several years before I became a Christian, my parents found Alcoholics Anonymous, and finally got sober. Shortly thereafter, I had the privilege of leading my mother and father to the Lord. Eventually my two brothers and two sisters became Christians.

Now, my parents grew up in the Catholic Church, but they never knew a person could become "born again" and have a life changing encounter with Jesus Christ. Once my parents gave their lives to Jesus, they decided that they would start a "born again/spirit-filled" addiction recovery group. They devoted the rest of their lives to starting Regeneration, meetings for people who needed to get freedom from addictions.

Mom and Dad started groups all over the East Coast of Australia. They began leading groups in prisons. They launched Regeneration groups in Russia and Siberia, and at Hillsong Church in Sydney, Australia, and at Wave Church, in Virginia Beach. Over the years, my parents helped hundreds of people break free from addiction and enter a personal relationship with Jesus Christ.

Eventually, my mother passed away, and Dad remained, on his own, dedicated to helping rescue people from addictions. He said, "As long as I'm alive, there are people to rescue, people to save. The devil used to beat me with this stick of addiction; now I'm going to beat him."

My father was in his later days, long past age 40, yet he knew the power of Jesus and he remained determined to hang onto God's promises until the very end.

As his life was nearing its end, and he was in a wheelchair, with oxygen, he continued to bring people to Christ. I was called to come to Australia once because the doctors said he was dying. When I walked into the hospital room, after an all-day flight, my Dad was sitting up in the bed, eating a boiled egg!

We were always joking with each other, so I said, "Hey, you're supposed to be dead."

He started to laugh. Then he started to cry as he said, "I can't help it, Steve. There are so many people who are still trapped in addiction. I wanted to go be with your mother, I heard the doctors saying that I wasn't going to make it but I remembered making God a promise that as long as I am alive I am going to devote my time to helping people break free from addiction."

And that's exactly what he did.

So miraculous was his strength to keep living and keep reaching the lost, the doctors called him "Lazarus", after the man in the New Testament who was resurrected by Jesus.

I happened to be in Australia, on vacation, when Dad called me. He was very sick and the doctors (this time) were sure he was not going to live much longer. Instead of worrying about himself or his condition, my Dad told me that he'd gotten his pastor to open the church on a night there wasn't a scheduled service, because I was going to preach.

Sure enough, Dad had invited everyone he was still working on to get free of addiction. He invited his nurse. He invited everyone he could – an old, sick man in a wheelchair – packed the church out!

While I was preaching, I told the audience that my father was my hero and I told them that my dad held onto life simply because he was believing for them to come to Jesus. That night, many people gave their life to Christ. Even my father's nurse gave her life to Christ, as well as many of the people he invited.

It was as if he had some people he wanted to reach for Jesus, and he wasn't going to die until he did. After the service, my dad pushed through the crowd in his wheelchair. He gave me a hug and said goodbye. I knew that he wasn't just saying goodbye for the evening, he was saying goodbye for good.

I went to his house shortly after that, and he was slipping in and out of consciousness. I walked in the room and took his hand. I told him, "If you can hear me, squeeze my hand." He squeezed my hand and I told him, "Dad, you're my hero. You can go on to be with Mom in Heaven. Many of the people you brought to church tonight accepted Christ."

I'm so proud of my father. On the last night of his life on Earth, he brought people into the Kingdom of God. He truly is my hero and my inspiration for reaching the lost.

At my father's funeral, for the first time ever, my son Josh spoke publicly. During that experience, Josh realized that God was calling him to preach. It was a life-changing moment. Now, Josh is the High School Youth Pastor of Wave Church and an extraordinary soul winner. Even after Dad was dead, he was having an impact for the Kingdom of God!

Though his start was rough, and his early life was plagued

with problems, William Kelly never let go of God's promises. Once he discovered Jesus, he lived for Him with his whole heart. For his incredible legacy and dedication to reaching the lost, William Kelly, my father, is a first-ballot member of the Caleb Generation.

7. Keep Fighting

As Chapter 6 explained, God's promises are a powerful "fountain of youth". If you have unfulfilled promises in your life, believe God will bring them to reality. You may, like Caleb, have to fight for your land, however.

Sometimes, the experience of fighting for a long time is a necessary one. It builds patience, wisdom and fortitude. When I think about the value of a long-term building of knowledge, I'm reminded of the story that's told in a variety of ways, but is a perfect illustration for the power of a Caleb Generation member who has stayed at the wheel, learning all the way.

The story goes that a man's car was making a terrible noise and he took it to a mechanic. The old mechanic had been working on cars since before automatic transmissions were mainstream.

The old-timer, after a couple minutes listening to the car, lifts the hood and finger tightens a screw deep in the engine compartment.

He then hands the customer an invoice for $300.

The customer is shocked and he questions the mechanic. "Three hundred dollars!" he declares, "For turning one screw. I could have done that for nothing! How can you justify this charge?"

The old mechanic slowly wipes his hands and tucks the dirty cloth in his back pocket. He reaches out and takes the invoice. He scribbles on it for a couple of seconds and hands it back to the customer.

The customer nods his head as he reads and reluctantly pulls out his wallet to pay the bill. What did the revised invoice say?

"$1.00 for turning the screw.
$299.00 for knowing which screw to turn."

The power of experience should not be underestimated. Like Caleb had to keep fighting, that old mechanic had probably turned many wrong screws in the years of trial-and-error before he reached the level of confidence that he had when fixing the man's car.

Forty-five years before he entered the Promised Land, Caleb saw the Canaanites and knew there would be a battle. God promised the territory to Israel, but they still had to evict the intruders.

While the Jews wandered in the desert for over four decades, the giants in the Promised Land remained. They built families and communities. They ate of the good of the land. They lived and populated. Whenever Israel finally entered the land, they still had to evict the intruders.

Caleb was old now, but his passion remained. His heart was strong and his strength was not reduced. He knew the fight would still be there, and that he would have to fight to claim God's Promised Land. This was clearly no problem for Caleb. I imagine he had so much built-up adrenaline from having to wander about the desert, all the while knowing the Promised Land was out there, that he could have taken the whole territory of the people like Samson, with a donkey jawbone.[30]

Here's what he says in Joshua 14:11-12, about finally being released to receive God's promise:

...So here I am today, eighty-five years old! I am still as strong today as the day Moses sent me out; I'm just as vigorous to go out to battle now as I was then. Now give me this hill country that God promised me that day. *You yourself heard then that the Anakites were there and their cities were large and fortified, but, the Lord helping me, I will drive them out just as He said.*"

I can picture him with his fist balled up, his knees flexed, bouncing on his toes. He probably would have knocked out George Foreman! Caleb was champing at the bit. He was lit up with the proximity of his vision. He had continued to fight, and was ready to fight, because God had made the promise.

This is a powerful inspiration. We are to keep fighting, no matter how long it takes, no matter the wilderness in which we are forced to wander. Caleb had to trudge about a real desert with a bunch of whiners and complainers and he never stopped fighting. He truly fought the good fight of faith, as the apostle Paul encouraged Timothy to do in the New Testament.

"Fight the good fight of faith. Take hold of the eternal life to which you were called when you made your good confession in the presence of many witnesses."[31]

This word is for the *Caleb Generation* as much as anyone. Paul provides a list of attributes to pursue, which enable us to achieve a good fight of faith. In 1 Timothy 6:11, he instructs Timothy to follow after the following:

- RIGHTEOUSNESS
- GODLINESS
- FAITH
- LOVE
- ENDURANCE
- GENTLENESS

These characteristics will support you as you fight the good fight of faith. If you pursue the above in your life, you will be able, like Caleb, to keep fighting. **And, when you do, one day you'll be standing on the border of your Promised Land. On that day, it won't matter what kind of giants are before you. Because you've fought the good fight of faith, you'll win. Because God has promised it to you, you'll take your land.**

Samuel Moore Walton[32]
(1918-1992)

Samuel Moore Walton, the founder of Wal-Mart, a child of the Depression, lived in various communities in the Midwest and Florida during his childhood. A highlight of his early years was obtaining the rank of Eagle Scout in the Boy Scouts as an eighth grader. He was clearly a young man with large ambitions.

After he left home, he attended the University of Missouri, and upon graduation, took a position with the JC Penney company. He served in the Army Intelligence Corps during World War II, eventually reaching the rank of captain.

After the war, as a 26-year-old, he bought a Ben Franklin variety store, with a $20,000 loan from his father-in-law plus $5,000 of his own money. Over the course of the next ten years, he grew his business and obtained additional stores. He was a retail innovator and he continually worked on his business concepts, always dedicated to the customer service and value that have come to be the hallmarks of the modern WalMart experience.

It wasn't all peaches and cream, however. In the late 1950s, he had a vision for a significantly different operation from the small "five-and-dime" stores that he owned. He proposed his giant retail concept, in rural communities, to the management of Ben Franklin stores. They laughed him out of the office.

Yet, Sam Walton refused to be denied. He was fifty years old now, but he was committed to seeing his vision come to pass. He kept fighting and fighting, and for the entire 1960s, he stayed one step ahead of his competition by expansion and acquisition.

According to his daughter, the only way they kept the mortgage paid for one building was to open another store and use the profits to pay the first debt. On and on he went, leveraging and fighting to build the company that is now the largest employer in the United States.

When Mr. Walton was first rejected by his management, he could have just resigned himself to accept his fate. He had decent success already. He had a chain of small stores and made good money. But it wasn't good enough. His mind was fixed and he fought until it became a reality.

For his ability and willingness to keep fighting, Sam Walton is a true member of the *Caleb Generation*.

8. Take Your Mountain

Caleb stood on the brink of entering God's promises. He had planned his battles. He lived with courage to swim against the tide. He knew the power of negativity. He kept his passion. He was willing to go; indeed, he went. He was young and strong because of God's promises. He never stopped fighting.

Now, after all those years, he was going to finally take his mountain. As he prepared to take the mountain, the hill country that he had seen forty-five years earlier, it's easy to imagine that he perceived it not only for himself, but for his family. For his children and his grandchildren, and beyond. This would be a place that would be their Promised Land forever.

The Bible says, in Joshua 14:13-14, *"Then Joshua blessed Caleb...and gave him Hebron as his inheritance. So Hebron has belonged to Caleb...ever since, because he followed the Lord, the God of Israel, wholeheartedly."*

The verse states that Hebron has belonged to Caleb (and thus his descendants) *ever since*. When you take a mountain, when you claim a promise of God, it's not for you alone. It's for the generations to come. It's for unborn children that you will never see. But you will be remembered.

I imagine Caleb's great-great-great grandchildren grew up hearing about his faith. They learned about his boldness and his passion. They were told great stories of how Caleb believed in God, and now the entire family was living in the blessing that came from Caleb, who stood alone and followed after God wholeheartedly.

What an amazing legacy. For Caleb, though the promise took a long time to manifest, the wait was worth it. **A *Caleb Generation* person may be delayed, but will not be denied.**

A key part of overcoming delay and patiently waiting to take your mountain is the revelation that the mountain is not only for you. The promises that God has made, even though years have gone by, are worth waiting for because the blessing of God will accrue to the benefit of hundreds and thousands of descendants that are yet to be born.

Caleb took his mountain, and it was a great piece of land. His offspring and their children and grandchildren lived in prime real estate. You see, in Joshua 14:15, the land given to Caleb was described as belonging to "Arba, who was the greatest among the Anakites."

In those days, land was taken by might, and it's not a difficult logical leap to make to assume that since Arba was the greatest among the people who inhabited the land before Caleb took it, the land was likely the best.

Caleb made it this far, and when the time came to take his mountain, it didn't matter if the people living there had super powers, he was coming for his land.

In life, as a member of the *Caleb Generation*, you will experience delay. You will learn to wait much longer than you'd hoped for dreams to come to pass. You will develop the staying power of Caleb, who wandered in the wilderness for forty years yet never abandoned God's promise for him and his family.

Remember that when it's time to take your mountain, you may still have to fight some giants. But you can do it, because your cause is bigger than yourself. In church life, when mountains are wrestled for the advancement of the Kingdom of God, the fight will be fierce and it will be hard. But the members of the *Caleb Generation will fight the good fight, and they will be victorious. Because not only are they conquering the land for themselves, they are taking what God has promised for the generations to come.*

The steps to membership in the *Caleb Generation* are listed below. Follow them and take your mountain. For yourself, but more importantly, for the generations waiting for their mountain!

Plan Your Battles

Swim Against the Tide

Understand Negativity

Keep Your Passion

GO

Trust God's Promises

Keep Fighting

(Endnotes)

1	Joshua 14:7
2	Exodus 12:40
3	Exodus 14
4	Genesis 12
5	Numbers 13
6	Numbers 13:31
7	Numbers 13:30
8	Numbers 20:12
9	http://www.granthomepage.com/grantchronology.htm
10	http://faculty.css.edu/mkelsey/usgrant/quotes.html
11	Joshua 14:7
12	Strong's Concordance H3824
13	Hebrews 11:6
14	http://www.imdb.com/name/nm0286040/bio
15	Numbers 14:8-9
16	Numbers 14:10
17	Numbers 14:12
18	Numbers 14:22-25
19	Proverbs 22:10
20	http://www.biography.com/people/cs-lewis-9380969
21	Miller, Laura. *The Magician's Book: A Skeptic's Ad ventures in Narnia, pp. 223*
22	Ibid, *pp. 76*

23   Joshua 14:10-11

24   http://www.tolkiensociety.org/tolkien/biography.html

25   2007 estimate. Provided by Vit Wagner, staff reporter, *Toronto Star,* April 16, 2007

26   http://www.biography.com/people/neil-arm strong-9188943

27   Genesis 12:2

28   Joshua 14:10

29   Genesis 37-50

30   Judges 15:16

31   1 Timothy 6:12

32   *Sam Walton biography,* CNBC: http://video.cnbc.com/gallery/?video=1248908415

About the Author

Steve Kelly is the Senior Pastor of Wave Church, a Christian church with national and international influence. Wave Church's two main campuses are in Virginia Beach, Virginia. It has multi-site campuses located throughout the state of Virginia, as well as North Carolina, with more to come.

Pastor Steve's passion is to win the lost and to lead the generations to find their purpose in Christ, through the building of the local church. Wave Church's primary mission is to help people do life well and find their purpose in Christ through being planted in the local church.

Made in the USA
Middletown, DE
24 June 2016